The Metaverse for Seniors

From Virtual Realities to Real Happiness

Caleb Watson

Table of Contents

Chapter 1: Introduction

Welcome to a remarkable journey into the future—the Metaverse! Imagine a vast digital world where imagination knows no bounds, where the line between reality and fantasy blurs, and where, as a senior, you hold the key to unlocking a world of endless possibilities.

1.1 The Metaverse: An Overview

Welcome to the Metaverse, a dazzling digital world that might just be the most exciting place you've never visited - yet! Picture it as a vast, interconnected playground where the real and the virtual converge, creating a space limited only by our imaginations.

Why It's So Exciting:

The Metaverse isn't your everyday internet. It's like stepping into your favorite science fiction novel, where you can explore distant worlds, meet people from all corners of the globe, and even defy the laws of physics - all from the comfort of your own home. It's a place where dreams come alive, and where you can be anyone or anything you want to be.

Personal Touch:

Now, you might be thinking, "This sounds like something for the tech-savvy young crowd." Well, think again! The Metaverse is for everyone, regardless of age. In fact, seniors bring a wealth of life experience and wisdom to this digital wonderland. It's a place where your unique perspective matters, and where you can engage with the world in entirely new ways.

What to Expect:

In this book, we'll take you by the hand and guide you through the Metaverse's magical landscape. We'll show you how to navigate, create your own digital persona (called an avatar), and introduce you to the incredible possibilities it offers. You don't need to be a computer expert to join the fun - just an open mind and a sense of adventure.

1.2 Why Seniors Matter in the Metaverse

Let's talk about why seniors, like you, are not just welcome but truly important in the Metaverse. This isn't just another tech trend; it's a digital realm where your presence can make a profound impact.

Your Experience Matters:
First and foremost, your life experiences, knowledge, and wisdom are incredibly valuable. Think of the Metaverse as a vast library, and you are one of its most treasured books. Your stories, your insights, and your unique perspective on the world are like gold in this digital age. You can share your experiences and connect with people from all walks

of life, enriching the Metaverse in ways only you can.

Building a Diverse Community:

The Metaverse thrives on diversity, and that includes age diversity. When seniors join, it becomes a more inclusive and vibrant space. You can bridge generational gaps, offer guidance, and inspire others with your journey through life. You'll find that your presence in the Metaverse contributes to building a richer and more varied community.

Learning and Growing Together:

The Metaverse isn't just about leisure; it's also a place for learning and personal growth. Seniors can participate in lifelong education, sharing their knowledge and, at the same time, gaining new skills and insights. It's a mutual exchange that benefits everyone involved.

Stay Social and Combat Isolation:

As we age, maintaining social connections becomes increasingly important. Loneliness and isolation can be real challenges, but the Metaverse provides a remedy. Here, you can make new friends, attend virtual gatherings, and strengthen existing relationships, all from the comfort of your home.

Leaving a Digital Legacy:

Your presence in the Metaverse isn't just for today; it's for tomorrow too. By engaging in this digital frontier, you're leaving a legacy for future generations. Your stories and contributions can inspire others long after you're gone.

Embrace the Adventure:

So, why do seniors matter in the Metaverse? Because you bring depth, wisdom, and a sense of adventure to this digital wonderland. Your presence enriches the experience for everyone, and your journey in the Metaverse can be an extraordinary adventure filled with learning, connection, and, most importantly, joy.

Next Up:

In the following chapters, we'll explore how you can make the most of your time in the Metaverse. From healthcare to entertainment, there's a world of possibilities waiting for you. So, are you ready to dive in and discover the endless wonders of the Metaverse? Let's continue this incredible journey together.

Chapter 2: Understanding the Metaverse

Welcome to the heart of the Metaverse! In this chapter, we're going to uncover the fascinating backstory of this digital wonderland and explore the very building blocks that make it possible. Get ready for a journey through time and technology that will leave you amazed at how we've reached this point.

Have you ever wondered how the Metaverse came to be? Well, you're not alone! It's a tale filled with innovation, visionary thinkers, and a dash of science fiction brought to life. We'll break it down in a way that's easy to understand because, in the Metaverse, the more you know, the more incredible it becomes.

2.1 A Brief History of the Metaverse

Welcome to the past, where the future was born!

Let's embark on a journey through time to uncover the exciting history of the Metaverse. It's a story of imagination, innovation, and the relentless pursuit of creating a digital realm where the impossible becomes possible.

The Early Seeds of Imagination: Our story begins in the minds of science fiction visionaries. Back in the 1930s, writers like Stanley G. Weinbaum and their tales of virtual reality set the stage for what was to come. They dared to dream of worlds beyond our own, sparking the imaginations of generations to come.

Enter the Cyberpunks: Fast forward to the 1980s and 1990s, the era of cyberpunk. Authors like

William Gibson envisioned a future where the digital and physical worlds would blend seamlessly. Their novels, like "Neuromancer," painted a vivid picture of a "Matrix"-like reality, where people could jack into a virtual universe.

The Birth of Virtual Worlds: In the early 1990s, virtual worlds like "Second Life" and "The Palace" emerged. These were the first glimpses of what we now recognize as the Metaverse. They allowed people to create digital personas, interact with others, and even buy virtual real estate. It was the dawn of a new era.

The Metaverse Takes Shape: As technology advanced, so did the Metaverse. Online gaming worlds like "World of Warcraft" and social spaces like "Club Penguin" captured the imaginations of millions. These platforms were precursors to the grand vision of a fully immersive Metaverse, where you could work, play, and socialize, all in one interconnected space.

Now that you've taken a trip through time, isn't it fascinating to see how these early seeds of imagination have sprouted into the Metaverse we know today? But the journey is far from over. In the next section, we'll dive into the technology that powers this digital universe, turning dreams into reality. Are you ready to explore the inner workings of the Metaverse?

2.2 The Building Blocks: VR, AR, and More

Welcome to the Metaverse's toolbox!

In this section, we're going to unravel the technological marvels that form the very foundation of the Metaverse. Think of these as the magic wands that transform your digital adventures into immersive experiences you can see, touch, and feel.

Virtual Reality (VR):

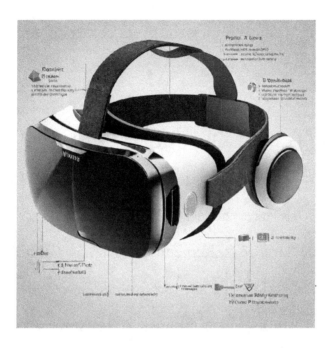

First, let's talk about VR, or Virtual Reality. Imagine putting on a special headset, and suddenly you're not in your living room anymore—you're in a completely different world! VR creates a 3D, computer-generated environment that you can explore as if you're really there. It's like stepping into a dream, and it's one of the cornerstones of the Metaverse.

Augmented Reality (AR):

Now, let's switch gears to Augmented Reality, or AR. AR takes the real world around you and adds a digital layer to it. Remember Pokémon GO? That's AR in action. It's like having hidden treasures and information superimposed onto your everyday surroundings. AR is all about enhancing your real-world experience with digital elements.

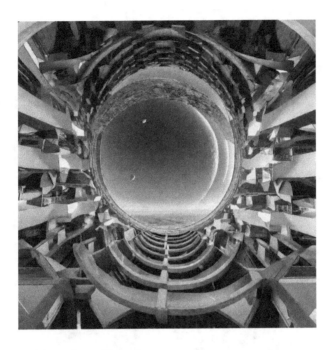

Mixed Reality (MR):

But wait, there's more! Mixed Reality, or MR, is where things get even more exciting. MR blends the real world with digital elements, just like AR, but it goes a step further. With MR, you can interact with those digital objects as if they're really there. It's like having holograms that you can touch and manipulate in your physical space.

Haptic Feedback and Beyond:

To make the Metaverse even more immersive, we have haptic feedback. Ever played a game where your controller vibrates when something exciting happens? Haptic feedback lets you feel sensations in the virtual world, adding another layer of realism. Plus, there are devices like gloves that let you touch and feel virtual objects.

Personalizing Your Experience:

The Metaverse also thrives on personalization. Devices like motion-tracking sensors and eye-tracking technology understand your movements and where you're looking. They make your digital avatar move and react just like you do in real life, making the Metaverse feel like an extension of yourself.

Now that you've got a glimpse into the tools behind the Metaverse's magic, aren't you excited to see how they come together to create incredible experiences? In the next chapters, we'll explore how you can use these technologies to step into the Metaverse and start your own adventure. What will you do first? Turn the page and let's find out!

Chapter 3: Navigating the Metaverse

Welcome to the Metaverse, the land of endless possibilities! In this chapter, we'll be your guides as we take our first steps into this digital wonderland. Buckle up and prepare to discover how to navigate this exciting realm, starting with crafting your digital identity.

Have you ever dreamed of being someone else, somewhere else, even if just for a little while? Well, the Metaverse is where those dreams come true. We'll show you how to become whoever you want to be, create your own virtual persona, and then dive into the heart of this digital universe.

3.1 Creating Your Digital Identity: Avatars and Customization

Welcome to the fun part of the Metaverse!

In this section, we're going to show you how to create your digital alter ego - your avatar. It's like designing your own action figure, but in the digital world. Get ready to let your imagination run wild!

Avatar Magic: Your avatar is your virtual representative, your digital twin in the Metaverse. It's how you'll appear to others, and it's a fantastic opportunity to be whoever you want to be. Want to be an adventurer, a scientist, a fashionista, or a combination of them all? Your avatar can embody your wildest dreams.

Starting from Scratch: Creating your avatar is a bit like sculpting with digital clay. You begin with a basic template, and from there, you can tweak every detail. Change your avatar's appearance, from their facial features to their clothing style. You're the artist, and your canvas is the Metaverse.

Express Yourself: One of the most exciting aspects of avatar creation is the freedom to express yourself. If you've always wanted to try a different hairstyle, experiment with bold fashion choices, or even turn back the clock to a younger version of yourself, here's your chance. Your avatar can reflect your style, your personality, or even your sense of humor.

Customization Galore: The options for customization are vast. You can choose from an array of hairstyles, skin tones, eye colors, and body types. And don't forget accessories! From hats to tattoos, you can add personal touches that make your avatar uniquely yours.

3.2 How to Access and Interact

Welcome to the gateway of the Metaverse!

Now that you've crafted your digital identity, your avatar, it's time to take that first exciting step into this vibrant digital realm. In this section, we'll show you how to access the Metaverse and navigate its virtual spaces. Get ready for an adventure like no other!

Entering the Metaverse: Congratulations! You're about to embark on a thrilling journey into the heart of the Metaverse. It's a digital realm where your dreams and interests can take center stage. But how do you get there? Don't worry; it's easier than you might think.

Device of Your Choice: First things first, you'll need the right device to access the Metaverse. There are options for every comfort level and preference. If you have a computer, you're already halfway there. You can also dive in using a virtual reality (VR) headset for a more immersive experience. Don't have a VR headset? No problem! Many Metaverse platforms offer mobile apps, so you can join in using your smartphone or tablet.

Creating Your Account: Just like with any online service, you'll need to create an account. This is your digital passport to the Metaverse. You'll choose a username, set a password, and provide some basic information. It's a straightforward process, and we'll guide you every step of the way to ensure your account is secure.

Exploring the Metaverse: Once you're in, the Metaverse becomes your digital playground. It's a world filled with endless possibilities. You'll start in a central hub or a welcome area where you can get your bearings. From there, you can choose your own adventure. Visit virtual museums, explore beautiful landscapes, attend live events, or even hang out with friends in digital social spaces.

Navigating Virtual Spaces:

Now that you've entered the Metaverse, it's time to explore the myriad of virtual spaces it has to offer.

Think of these spaces as the different realms within a massive digital universe. Each one holds unique adventures, experiences, and opportunities waiting for you to discover.

Selecting Your Destination: Just like choosing your next vacation spot, you can select where you want to go in the Metaverse. Want to visit a serene virtual beach, explore a bustling city, or enter a sci-fi adventure? The choices are virtually limitless. You can browse through a catalog of virtual worlds, events, and experiences to decide where you'd like to go next.

Moving About: Navigating these virtual spaces is surprisingly easy. You can typically move your avatar using your keyboard or controller if you're on a computer, or through body movements if you're in VR. Walking, flying, and even teleporting are common methods of getting around. You'll quickly get the hang of it and be zipping from one virtual place to another in no time.

Interacting with Objects: In the Metaverse, you're not just a passive observer; you're an active participant. You can interact with objects and elements within these virtual worlds. Touching, picking up, or manipulating items can be as simple as a click or a gesture, depending on your device. This interactivity makes the Metaverse feel like a living, breathing space.

Connecting with Others: One of the most exciting aspects of virtual spaces is the opportunity to meet and connect with people from all over the world. You can strike up conversations, make new friends, or collaborate on projects just like you would in real life. It's a space where social interactions are limited only by your imagination.

Endless Discoveries: Virtual spaces within the Metaverse are as diverse as the real world itself. From virtual museums and educational simulations to entertainment zones and social gatherings, there's always something new to explore. The more you venture, the more you'll uncover, and the richer your experience will become.

Interacting with Others:

One of the most captivating aspects of the Metaverse is the opportunity to connect and engage with people from all corners of the globe. It's like attending a never-ending digital party, and you're invited! In this section, we'll guide you through the exciting world of social interactions within the Metaverse.

Meeting New People: Just like at a social gathering in the real world, the Metaverse is a place where you can meet new people and make friends. Whether you strike up a conversation at a virtual cafe, join a discussion group, or attend a virtual concert, there are countless opportunities to connect. You'll find that the Metaverse is a diverse and welcoming space with individuals of all ages, backgrounds, and interests.

Building Digital Relationships: As you spend more time in the Metaverse, you may find that your digital connections become meaningful friendships. You can communicate through text chat, voice chat, or even video chat, just like you would in real life.

Share stories, experiences, and interests with people who share your passions or introduce you to new ones.

Collaboration and Creativity: Beyond casual interactions, the Metaverse is a hub for collaboration and creativity. You can work on projects, attend workshops, or join creative communities. Imagine designing virtual worlds, collaborating on art projects, or even coding together with like-minded individuals.

Enhancing Real-Life Relationships: The Metaverse also offers opportunities to enhance existing relationships. You can stay connected with friends and family who might be physically distant, and you can share experiences together in a virtual space. It's a way to bridge the gap between physical and digital worlds.

Digital Gatherings and Events: One of the most exciting aspects of the Metaverse is the abundance of virtual events and gatherings. You can attend concerts, conferences, and even weddings—all from the comfort of your digital avatar. These events often feature live performances, interactive experiences, and a chance to connect with people who share your interests.

It's All About You:

In the Metaverse, your preferences and comfort are at the forefront. It's a space where you can tailor your experiences to suit your interests, desires, and needs. Here, the Metaverse truly becomes an extension of yourself.

Personalization is Key: One of the most appealing aspects of the Metaverse is its flexibility. Whether you're a tech-savvy senior or someone new to digital spaces, you can customize your experience to match your comfort level. You decide how deep you want to dive into this digital universe.

Choose Your Path: In the Metaverse, you're in control. You can decide how you want to spend your time. Whether it's exploring virtual worlds, attending live events, or engaging in social interactions, the choice is yours. There's no right or wrong way to experience the Metaverse—it's about what brings you joy.

Your Digital Persona: Remember that avatar you created? It's not just a digital representation; it's an extension of yourself in this virtual world. You can change it, modify it, and experiment with it whenever you like. Want to try a new look or theme for the day? Go for it! Your avatar is your canvas.

Privacy and Safety: Your safety and privacy are paramount in the Metaverse. Most platforms have robust privacy settings, so you can control who can interact with you and how much information you share. It's essential to familiarize yourself with these settings to ensure a safe and enjoyable experience.

Social or Solo Adventures: Whether you're a social butterfly or prefer solo adventures, the Metaverse caters to your style. You can join bustling virtual gatherings, participate in group activities, or explore serene virtual landscapes on your own. It's a space where introverts and extroverts alike can thrive.

Now that you know it's all about you in the Metaverse, how will you choose to shape your digital journey? The possibilities are endless, and the adventure is yours to craft. In the upcoming chapters, we'll delve deeper into the ways seniors can benefit from the Metaverse, from healthcare to education and beyond. What will your Metaverse experience look like? Turn the page and let's continue exploring this vibrant digital realm together!

Chapter 4: Benefits for Seniors

Welcome to the chapter that dives deep into how the Metaverse can transform the lives of seniors. It's not just about virtual adventures; it's about enhancing your well-being and connecting with others like never before. In this chapter, we'll explore the fantastic ways the Metaverse can make a positive impact on your life.

Have you ever imagined a world where you can improve your health, well-being, and social connections, all while having fun? Well, that world is real, and it's called the Metaverse. Get ready to discover how this digital realm can lead to a happier, healthier, and more fulfilling life for seniors.

4.1 Health and Wellness in the Metaverse

Welcome to your digital wellness sanctuary!

The Metaverse isn't just about virtual adventures; it's also a place where you can take significant steps toward improving your health and well-being. Imagine having access to a world of wellness right at your fingertips.

Your Personal Wellness Oasis:

Imagine starting your day in the Metaverse with the sun rising over a tranquil mountain range. The chirping of virtual birds welcomes you to your personal wellness sanctuary. In this digital realm, your well-being is a top priority, and we're here to guide you through the possibilities.

Meditation for Inner Peace: Stress melts away as you join guided meditation sessions led by experts in serene virtual environments. Picture yourself sitting by a virtual waterfall, the sound of cascading water soothing your soul. These sessions are designed to help you find inner peace, reduce anxiety, and promote mental clarity.

Yoga in Stunning Settings: Feel the virtual breeze on your skin as you join a yoga class set against breathtaking backdrops. Stretch and breathe in lush virtual forests or on tranquil virtual beaches. Yoga in the Metaverse isn't just about physical exercise; it's about connecting with nature and yourself. It's a holistic approach to wellness.

Immersive Fitness Adventures: If you're a fitness enthusiast, the Metaverse has thrilling options. Dive into immersive fitness games where you'll jog through digital jungles, punch virtual targets, or dance your way to fitness. These experiences not only keep you physically active but also make exercise genuinely enjoyable.

Connecting with Wellness Communities: In the Metaverse, you're never alone on your wellness journey. Join communities of like-minded individuals who share your wellness goals. Whether it's a virtual support group for managing health conditions or a fitness club for staying active, these communities offer camaraderie and motivation.

Connecting with Healthcare Professionals:

In the Metaverse, your access to healthcare takes on a new dimension, making it more convenient and accessible than ever before. Picture a world where healthcare professionals are just a virtual appointment away, and your well-being is within your control.

Virtual Doctor Visits: The Metaverse brings healthcare right to your doorstep. Through telemedicine services, you can schedule virtual appointments with doctors and specialists. It's as simple as logging into a virtual clinic from the comfort of your home. Whether it's a routine check-up, a follow-up, or a consultation about a specific health concern, you can receive expert guidance without the need for travel.

Consulting Specialists: No matter where you are, the Metaverse connects you to specialists who can provide expert insights into your health. From dermatologists to mental health professionals, specialists are accessible through virtual consultations. This means you can get the care and attention you need, even for specific health conditions or concerns.

Convenience and Efficiency: Virtual healthcare appointments in the Metaverse are designed for efficiency. There's no need to spend time commuting to a physical clinic or waiting in crowded waiting rooms. Your appointments start on time, and you can discuss your health concerns from the comfort of your own space.

Health Records and Monitoring: Many Metaverse healthcare platforms offer tools to keep track of your health records and monitor your well-being. You can securely access your medical history, test results, and treatment plans. This empowers you to take an active role in managing your health.

The Metaverse is not just about leisure; it's a place where your health and well-being are prioritized. In the upcoming sections, we'll continue to explore how the Metaverse can positively impact your life, from overcoming loneliness to lifelong learning and beyond. How does the idea of convenient, accessible healthcare in the Metaverse sound to you?

4.2 Overcoming Loneliness and Isolation

Loneliness and isolation can be tough challenges, especially for seniors. But what if we told you that the Metaverse has the power to transform these struggles into a distant memory? In this section, we'll explore how the Metaverse offers a lifeline of connection, turning isolation into a thing of the past.

Imagine having a vibrant social life, even if you're physically distant from friends and family. In the Metaverse, this isn't just a dream—it's a reality. We'll delve deep into how the digital world can help you combat loneliness, build meaningful connections, and enrich your social life.

Combating Loneliness:

Virtual Social Groups: The Metaverse is teeming with virtual social groups that cater to a wide range of interests. Whether you're passionate about gardening, book clubs, art, or a particular hobby, you can find like-minded individuals who share your enthusiasm. Joining these groups is as easy as clicking a button. It's like attending a gathering of friends who understand your interests and passions.

Digital Hangouts with Friends: Reconnecting with old friends and making new ones is just a click away in the Metaverse. You can invite friends or family members to join you in virtual hangouts.

These digital gatherings allow you to spend quality time together, even if you're miles apart. Share stories, play games, or simply chat as if you're in the same room.

Building Meaningful Connections: Social interactions in the Metaverse are not limited to superficial conversations. You can engage in deep and meaningful discussions, forming bonds that can be just as strong as those forged in the physical world. It's a space where friendships can flourish and emotional connections can be nurtured.

Fostering Social Connections:

Participating in Virtual Events: The Metaverse hosts a plethora of virtual events, from concerts to art exhibitions, where you can immerse yourself in shared experiences. These events are designed to bring people together and foster a sense of community. Imagine attending a live concert with thousands of virtual attendees, all there to enjoy the music and connect with others.

Digital Gatherings and Celebrations: Special occasions, holidays, and celebrations are not limited by physical boundaries in the Metaverse. You can host virtual parties, celebrate birthdays, and attend digital weddings. It's a way to be part of significant life moments, no matter where you or your loved ones are located.

Are you excited about the potential of the Metaverse to transform your social life and help you overcome loneliness? It's a world where connections are boundless, and isolation is a thing of the past. In the upcoming sections, we'll continue to explore how the Metaverse can enrich your life, from lifelong learning to entertainment and beyond. How do you envision your social life thriving in this digital wonderland? Turn the page, and let's keep uncovering the magic of the Metaverse together!

Chapter 5: Healthcare in the Metaverse

Healthcare in the Metaverse is not just innovative; it's revolutionary. Imagine accessing world-class medical expertise without leaving your home, or recovering from an injury through immersive virtual experiences. In this chapter, we'll explore the incredible ways the Metaverse is transforming healthcare, putting your well-being at the forefront.

Are you ready to embark on a journey that brings healthcare into the digital age? The Metaverse is more than just virtual adventures; it's a place where your health and wellness can thrive. Get ready to discover how this digital realm can lead to a healthier, happier you.

5.1 Virtual Doctor Visits: A New Frontier in Healthcare

Are you ready to step into a world where healthcare is as convenient as a click of a button? Virtual doctor visits in the Metaverse are not just innovative; they're a game-changer for your well-being. Let's explore how this digital realm can make healthcare more accessible and efficient for you.

Revolutionizing Healthcare Access:

The Metaverse Clinic: Picture this: you need medical advice, and instead of driving to a physical clinic, you log into a virtual one. The Metaverse clinic is your portal to healthcare. It's a place where you can schedule appointments, consult with healthcare professionals, and receive the medical care you need—all from the comfort of your home. No more worrying about traffic or waiting rooms.

Consulting Specialists: Health concerns can often require specialized expertise. In the Metaverse, you have access to a network of specialists. Whether it's a dermatologist, cardiologist, or any other specialist, you can schedule virtual appointments with ease. It's about receiving the right care from the right experts, regardless of geographical constraints.

Efficiency and Convenience: Virtual doctor visits prioritize your time and well-being. Your appointments start on time, reducing unnecessary waiting. Plus, you can access your medical records and test results digitally. This means you have a comprehensive view of your health, empowering you to make informed decisions about your well-being.

Cost-Effective Care: Traditional healthcare often comes with hidden costs, from transportation expenses to parking fees. In the Metaverse, you save both time and money. Virtual doctor visits can be more cost-effective, eliminating the need for commuting and additional expenses.

How does the idea of accessing healthcare expertise conveniently from your own home sound to you? The Metaverse clinic is open 24/7, and the future of healthcare is at your fingertips. In the following sections, we'll continue to explore how the Metaverse can enrich your life, from wellness to lifelong learning and beyond. How do you envision virtual doctor visits changing your healthcare experience?

5.2 Wellness and Rehabilitation in Virtual Spaces

Welcome to Your Digital Wellness Oasis:

In the Metaverse, your well-being is not just a priority; it's a transformative experience. Imagine starting your day with a guided meditation session set in a serene virtual environment. The gentle sounds of nature surround you as you find inner peace. This is the power of wellness and rehabilitation in virtual spaces, and we're about to dive into how it can enhance your life.

Your Personal Meditation Retreat: Stress and anxiety can often weigh us down. In the Metaverse, you have access to guided meditation sessions that take you to calming virtual locales. Imagine sitting by a virtual waterfall, the sound of flowing water soothing your soul. These sessions are designed to reduce stress, improve mental clarity, and enhance your overall sense of well-being. It's like having a peaceful retreat within reach, no matter where you are.

Yoga in Stunning Settings: Physical and mental well-being go hand in hand. Virtual yoga classes offer more than just a workout—they provide a holistic experience. Picture yourself stretching and breathing in lush virtual forests or on tranquil virtual beaches. It's not just exercise; it's a connection to nature and yourself. Wellness in the Metaverse is about nourishing your mind, body, and spirit.

Immersive Rehabilitation:

Recovery from injuries or surgeries can be challenging, but the Metaverse introduces a groundbreaking approach to rehabilitation that's as exciting as it is effective.

Virtual Rehabilitation Adventures: Imagine stepping into a world where rehabilitation exercises aren't mundane but immersive adventures. In the Metaverse, you can engage in therapeutic activities set in captivating virtual environments. Whether you're relearning to walk or regaining mobility in an injured limb, these exercises take you on exciting journeys. It's like playing a video game designed specifically for your recovery.

Personalized Progress Tracking:

The Metaverse doesn't just offer immersive exercises; it also provides tools for tracking your progress. You can monitor your rehabilitation journey in real-time, seeing how you're improving and achieving your milestones. It's a motivating way to stay on track and celebrate your achievements.

Guidance from Virtual Instructors:

In this virtual realm, you're not alone in your rehabilitation journey. Virtual instructors guide you through exercises, ensuring you perform them correctly and safely. They provide real-time feedback, making the process both educational and enjoyable. It's like having a personal trainer who's always by your side.

Interactive Support Communities: Recovery is often more manageable when you have a support network. In the Metaverse, you can join virtual rehabilitation communities filled with individuals who understand your journey. Share your challenges, successes, and tips with others who are on similar paths. It's a space for mutual encouragement and support.

Does the idea of immersive rehabilitation adventures sound appealing to you? The Metaverse transforms recovery into an engaging experience, and your health becomes an exciting journey. In the following sections, we'll continue to explore how the Metaverse can enhance your life, from lifelong learning to entertainment and beyond. How do you envision your rehabilitation journey in this digital wonderland? Turn the page, and let's keep discovering the potential of the Metaverse together!

Chapter 6: Social Connections

Welcome to the chapter that celebrates the joy of connections in the Metaverse. It's not just about virtual spaces; it's about rekindling old friendships, forging new bonds, and celebrating moments together. In this chapter, we'll delve into the magic of social connections and how the Metaverse can bring people closer, no matter the distance.

Picture this: you're in a bustling virtual cafe, sipping your favorite digital coffee, and chatting with friends from around the world. This is the essence of social connections in the Metaverse—a world where friendships thrive, gatherings come to life, and the sense of community knows no bounds. Get ready to explore the incredible ways the Metaverse enriches your social life.

6.1 Seniors Reconnect: Virtual Social Spaces

Rediscovering Old Friendships:

Have you ever thought about the friends from your past, those cherished connections that time or distance might have momentarily separated? In the Metaverse, these reunions are not just possible; they're within reach, and they can fill your life with joy and nostalgia.

Virtual Messages and Reconnect Requests: The journey to rediscovering old friendships starts with a digital message. You can reach out to those friends, send them a virtual hello, and express your desire to reconnect. It's as simple as typing a few heartfelt words and hitting send. The Metaverse bridges the gap between you and the people you've missed.

Planning a Virtual Reunion: Once you've rekindled the connection, the Metaverse offers a space to plan a virtual reunion. You can choose from a variety of virtual settings, from cozy cafes to picturesque parks. It's like organizing a gathering in the real world, but with a touch of digital magic. Invite your old friends, and together, you can create new memories while reminiscing about the past.

Sharing Stories and Memories: In these virtual reunions, the Metaverse becomes a canvas for storytelling and sharing memories. You can exchange stories about your lives, relive old adventures, and catch up on the latest news. It's a space where time seems to stand still, allowing you to reconnect on a profound level.

Joining Virtual Social Groups:

The Metaverse is a vast landscape of virtual social spaces where you can find a community that shares your passions and interests. It's a place where your hobbies and enthusiasms can flourish, and where making new friends who truly understand you is just a click away.

Exploring Diverse Communities: In the Metaverse, you're not limited by geographical constraints when seeking like-minded individuals. Whether you're passionate about gardening, astronomy, literature, or any other interest, there's likely a virtual social group for you. These communities are welcoming, diverse, and enthusiastic about their chosen topics.

Easy Access and Participation: Joining these groups is incredibly straightforward. With a few clicks, you can become a member of a virtual community. You'll have access to discussions, events, and activities related to your shared interest. It's like attending a gathering of friends who are as enthusiastic as you are.

Sharing Knowledge and Experiences: Virtual social groups in the Metaverse are hubs of knowledge exchange and shared experiences. Whether you're a novice or an expert in your interest area, you'll find a space where you can learn, contribute, and grow. These communities are fertile grounds for expanding your horizons and connecting with people who have similar passions.

Building Lasting Friendships: What makes virtual social groups in the Metaverse special is the potential for building genuine friendships. Shared interests provide a solid foundation for meaningful connections. Engaging in conversations, collaborating on projects, and participating in events can lead to friendships that transcend the digital realm.

6.2 Attending Events and Gatherings in the Metaverse:

Let's step into a world where the boundaries of geography and physical presence fade away, where events and gatherings take on new dimensions of excitement and possibility. In the Metaverse, attending events and celebrations isn't just about participation; it's about immersion, connection, and the thrill of shared experiences. Get ready to dive deep into how the Metaverse transforms the way we come together.

Picture this: you're attending a virtual concert, dancing with friends from different corners of the globe, and feeling the energy of the music as if you were in the front row. This is the essence of events and gatherings in the Metaverse—a world where distance is no obstacle, and community knows no borders. Let's explore how the Metaverse enhances your participation in celebrations and events.

The Thrill of Virtual Events:

Concerts, Art Exhibitions, and More: The Metaverse hosts a wide array of virtual events, from live music concerts by your favorite artists to art exhibitions showcasing the works of talented creators. These events are designed to transport you to new realms of excitement and creativity. You can immerse yourself in the music, art, and culture of these virtual gatherings.

Global Participation: One of the wonders of the Metaverse is its global reach. When you attend a virtual event, you're not limited by physical boundaries. Instead, you're sharing the experience with people from around the world who share your interests. It's like being part of a diverse and vibrant global community.

Interactivity and Engagement: Virtual events are not passive experiences. You can interact with the environment, chat with fellow attendees, and even participate in activities related to the event. For example, at a virtual art gallery, you can discuss the artwork with other attendees and the artists themselves. These interactions make the experience richer and more engaging.

Digital Gatherings and Celebrations:

Host Your Own Virtual Parties: The Metaverse empowers you to create your own digital gatherings and celebrations. Whether it's a birthday party, a family reunion, or just a casual get-together, you can host it virtually. Invite your friends and loved ones, and together you can celebrate life's special moments. It's a way to be together even when you're physically apart.

Unique Celebrations: Special occasions become even more memorable in the Metaverse. Imagine attending a virtual wedding where guests from around the world gather to witness the ceremony. Or perhaps you're celebrating a holiday with loved ones who are miles away. These unique celebrations create lasting memories and strengthen bonds.

Are you excited about the potential of attending events and gatherings in the Metaverse? It's a world where celebrations become more vibrant, events more interactive, and connections more profound. In the upcoming sections, we'll continue to explore how the Metaverse can enrich your life, from lifelong learning to entertainment and beyond.

What virtual event or celebration are you looking forward to attending in this digital wonderland? Turn the page, and let's keep unlocking the magic of the Metaverse together!

Chapter 7: Learning and Lifelong Education

Imagine a world where the pursuit of knowledge has no limits, where you can explore history, science, art, and culture from the comfort of your home. In the Metaverse, learning isn't confined to classrooms; it's a lifelong adventure filled with wonder and discovery. In this chapter, we'll embark on a journey through virtual classrooms, museums, and historical adventures, uncovering how the Metaverse redefines the way we learn.

Are you ready to step into a realm where learning is as engaging as it is boundless? The Metaverse is not just a place for leisure; it's a space where your thirst for knowledge can thrive. Get ready to explore how the digital world enhances your opportunities for education and lifelong learning.

7.1 Online Classes and Tutorials

In the Metaverse, the doors to learning are wide open, and the possibilities are endless. Whether you've always wanted to play a musical instrument, explore a new language, or delve into the mysteries of coding, the Metaverse offers a rich landscape of online classes and tutorials. Learning here isn't just a task; it's an adventure filled with excitement and growth.

Are you ready to embark on a journey of self-improvement and discovery? The Metaverse isn't just a playground for leisure; it's a thriving ecosystem of knowledge where your curiosity and aspirations can flourish. Let's dive deep into how online classes and tutorials in the Metaverse empower you to become the lifelong learner you've always wanted to be.

Unlocking the World of Online Learning:

Limitless Subjects and Topics: In the Metaverse, the spectrum of learning opportunities is vast. You can choose from a myriad of subjects and topics, from traditional subjects like mathematics and history to cutting-edge fields like artificial intelligence and virtual reality. It's like having a world-class library at your fingertips, where you can explore your interests and passions.

Personalized Learning Paths: Online classes and tutorials in the Metaverse are designed with your unique learning journey in mind. You can select courses that match your current skill level and learning pace. Whether you're a beginner, an intermediate learner, or an expert seeking mastery, there's a virtual classroom tailored just for you.

Accessible Anytime, Anywhere: The beauty of online learning in the Metaverse is its accessibility. You can access your courses and tutorials at any time, from anywhere with an internet connection. There are no fixed schedules or geographical constraints. It's like having a virtual school that accommodates your lifestyle.

Engaging Virtual Instructors:

Passionate Educators: In virtual classrooms, you're guided by passionate educators who bring their expertise to life. These instructors are not just experts in their fields; they're also skilled in creating engaging and immersive learning experiences. It's like having a mentor who's genuinely invested in your success.

Interactive Learning: Learning in the Metaverse is not a one-way street; it's an interactive journey. You can engage in hands-on activities, simulations, and discussions. Virtual classrooms are designed to make learning enjoyable and memorable. It's like stepping into the heart of the subject matter, where you can explore and experiment.

Community of Learners: You're not alone in your educational journey. Virtual classrooms in the Metaverse are bustling with fellow learners who share your interests and goals. It's a community where you can collaborate on projects, exchange ideas, and learn from one another. Learning becomes a collective adventure.

Connecting with Fellow Learners:

Learning in the Metaverse is not a solitary pursuit; it's a communal experience where you can connect with fellow learners who share your passions and ambitions. Here's how the Metaverse transforms learning into a social adventure:

Building a Network of Peers: In virtual classrooms and online learning communities, you'll encounter learners from diverse backgrounds and locations. These connections are a valuable asset in your learning journey. They can provide fresh perspectives, share insights, and even become friends who motivate and support you.

Collaboration on Projects: Many online courses in the Metaverse encourage collaborative projects and group activities. You can team up with fellow learners to tackle challenges, solve problems, and create something meaningful together. This collaborative spirit fosters a sense of camaraderie and helps you develop essential teamwork skills.

Discussion and Idea Exchange: Virtual classrooms often include discussion boards and forums where you can engage in conversations about course topics. These platforms are perfect for sharing your thoughts, asking questions, and exploring different viewpoints. It's a space where learning becomes a dynamic exchange of ideas.

Mentoring and Peer Support: In the Metaverse, you're not just learning from instructors; you can also benefit from the expertise of your peers. Some learners may have more experience in specific areas and can act as mentors or guides. Similarly, you can offer your knowledge to others. This mutual support system enriches the learning experience.

Celebrating Achievements Together: Learning in the Metaverse is not just about acquiring knowledge; it's also about celebrating achievements. Whether it's completing a challenging course, mastering a new skill, or accomplishing a group project, you can share your successes with your fellow learners. It's a space where every milestone is acknowledged and celebrated.

7.2 Virtual Museums and Historical Adventures

Step into the shoes of an adventurer and a historian, as we explore the wonders of virtual museums and historical adventures in the Metaverse. Here, history comes alive in ways you've never imagined, and the world's cultural treasures are within your reach. In this section, we'll embark on a journey through time and art, discovering how the Metaverse allows us to explore history and culture in thrilling and immersive ways.

Are you ready to journey back in time, walk among ancient civilizations, and witness art and culture like never before? The Metaverse isn't just a digital realm; it's a gateway to historical and cultural adventures that will leave you in awe. Let's dive deep into how virtual museums and historical experiences transport you to different eras and inspire a profound sense of wonder.

Exploring History and Culture:

Transporting to Ancient Civilizations: In the Metaverse, you can step back in time to visit ancient civilizations. Wander through the streets of ancient Rome, stand in the grandeur of the Egyptian pyramids, or explore the mysteries of the Mayan temples. These virtual recreations offer an authentic sense of what life was like in these bygone eras. It's like being a time traveler.

Front-Row Seats to Art and Masterpieces:
Virtual museums bring world-renowned artworks
to your screen. You can stand before masterpieces
by the likes of Leonardo da Vinci, Vincent van
Gogh, and Michelangelo. The level of detail and
immersion allows you to appreciate every

brushstroke and every nuance of these artworks. It's like having a private viewing with the artist.

Interactive Learning: These virtual experiences are not passive; they're interactive and educational. You can zoom in on artworks, examine historical artifacts up close, and even participate in interactive simulations. For instance, you can try your hand at deciphering hieroglyphics in an Egyptian tomb or restoring a Renaissance painting. Learning becomes an adventure of the senses.

Digital Reenactments and Historical Adventures:

The Metaverse doesn't just allow you to passively observe history; it invites you to step into the shoes of historical figures and participate in key events. Here's how digital reenactments and historical adventures in the Metaverse bring history to life:

Walking in the Shoes of Historical Figures: Imagine the thrill of assuming the roles of historical icons like Cleopatra, Galileo, or Amelia Earhart. In the Metaverse, you can do just that. Digital reenactments and historical adventures offer you a chance to experience pivotal moments in history through the eyes of those who lived them. You can immerse yourself in their stories, motivations, and challenges. It's like having a time machine that allows you to meet the great figures of the past.

Participation in Key Events: Some historical adventures in the Metaverse go beyond mere observation; they invite you to actively participate in significant historical events. For instance, you can join the Apollo 11 mission to the moon or be present at the signing of the Declaration of

Independence. These experiences let you not only witness history but also play a role in shaping it. It's like being part of a living history book where your actions matter.

Understanding Significance and Impact: By actively participating in historical events and reenactments, you gain a profound understanding of their significance and impact on the course of history. You can feel the weight of decisions made during critical moments and appreciate the bravery and sacrifices of those who came before us. It's a deeply moving and educational experience that fosters a connection with the past.

Are you excited about the opportunity to step into the shoes of historical figures and become an active participant in the events that shaped our world? The Metaverse offers you the chance to not only learn about history but to live it. In the following sections, we'll continue to uncover how the Metaverse can enrich your life, from entertainment to health and beyond. Which historical era or event are you most eager to explore and experience in this digital wonderland? Turn the page, and let's keep unlocking the magic of the Metaverse together!

Chapter 8: Entertainment and Recreation

Welcome to the most thrilling chapter yet—the gateway to boundless fun, adventure, and leisure in the Metaverse. Here, entertainment isn't just about escapism; it's about becoming the hero of your own story, exploring new worlds, and embracing your passions. In this chapter, we'll dive into the exhilarating realms of virtual travel and gaming, uncovering how the Metaverse revolutionizes the way we seek amusement and recreation.

Are you ready for an adventure like no other? The Metaverse isn't just a digital playground; it's a universe of possibilities where your imagination can take flight. Get ready to discover how entertainment in the Metaverse transcends the ordinary and makes the extraordinary a part of your everyday life.

8.1 Travel the World Virtually

Pack your virtual bags and get ready for an adventure like no other—the world of virtual travel in the Metaverse! It's time to explore the globe, visit iconic destinations, and immerse yourself in different cultures—all without leaving the comfort of your home. In this section, we'll take you on a journey through the wonders of virtual travel, where every day is a new expedition.

Are you ready to embark on a globe-trotting adventure from your living room? Virtual travel in the Metaverse isn't just about seeing new places; it's about experiencing them with all your senses. Get ready to discover how this digital wonderland can make your travel dreams a reality, anytime you desire.

Exploring the World from Your Home:

Boundless Destinations at Your Fingertips: In the Metaverse, your travel dreams know no bounds. Here's how virtual travel opens up a world of destinations that you can explore from the comfort of your home:

Endless Variety of Destinations: Imagine having access to a never-ending list of destinations, each with its unique charm and allure. In the Metaverse, you can choose where you want to go, whether it's the vibrant streets of Tokyo, the romantic canals of Venice, or the serene landscapes of Patagonia. It's like having a travel agency that offers you the entire world as your playground.

Personalized Adventures: Virtual travel in the Metaverse is a personalized experience. You can tailor your adventures to match your interests and preferences. If you're an architecture enthusiast, explore virtual cities and marvel at their iconic buildings. Nature lovers can hike through virtual national parks and witness breathtaking scenery. Foodies can embark on virtual culinary tours, sampling delicacies from around the globe. It's like curating your dream travel itinerary with limitless possibilities.

Accessible Exploration: The beauty of virtual travel is its accessibility. You can "visit" destinations that might be challenging to reach in real life due to physical limitations or logistical constraints. Climb the Himalayas without breaking a sweat, explore the Amazon rainforest without worrying about insects, or stroll through the historic streets of Pompeii without the crowds. It's like having a backstage pass to the world's most incredible places.

Realism and Immersion: Virtual travel isn't just about seeing static images; it's about immersing yourself in a lifelike environment. The Metaverse offers 360-degree experiences, allowing you to look around in all directions, creating a sense of presence. You can hear the sounds of your surroundings, from the chatter of a bustling market to the rustling leaves in a forest. It's like stepping into a postcard and feeling the world around you.

Immersive Cultural Experiences:

In the Metaverse, cultural immersion takes on a whole new dimension. Here's how virtual travel allows you to become a part of different cultures, creating experiences that are both educational and deeply enriching:

Authentic Cultural Festivals: Imagine being in the midst of vibrant cultural festivals from around the world, all from the comfort of your home. In the Metaverse, you can attend virtual celebrations, whether it's the colorful Carnival in Rio de Janeiro, the breathtaking lantern festival in Taiwan, or the lively Diwali celebrations in India. These experiences are not mere simulations; they capture the essence and energy of these events. It's like having a front-row seat to the world's most captivating celebrations.

Taste the World's Cuisines: Culinary exploration is a significant part of cultural immersion, and the Metaverse has you covered. You can virtually dine at international restaurants, sample diverse cuisines, and even learn to cook traditional dishes from different cultures. Taste the flavors of Japan with a sushi-making class, savor the spices of India with a cooking tutorial, or indulge in the delicacies of Italy with a virtual pasta-making experience. It's like having a world of cuisines at your fingertips.

Conversations with Locals: Cultural immersion isn't complete without interactions with locals. In the Metaverse, you can engage in conversations with digital residents who embody the culture of the places you visit. Ask questions, learn about their customs, and gain insights into their way of life. These interactions foster a deeper understanding of cultural nuances and create connections with people from around the world. It's like having a global cultural exchange without leaving your home.

Appreciation of Diversity: Through immersive cultural experiences, you develop a profound appreciation for the diversity of our world. You can explore the rich tapestry of traditions, art, music, and languages that make each culture unique. It's an opportunity to celebrate our shared humanity while embracing the beauty of our differences. It's like having a passport to the world's cultural heritage.

8.2 Gaming, Hobbies, and More:

Welcome to a world where your passions take center stage, your creativity knows no bounds, and your leisure time becomes an endless adventure. In this chapter, we'll dive into the thrilling realms of gaming, hobbies, and beyond in the Metaverse. Get ready to explore how the digital wonderland of the Metaverse transforms your hobbies and recreational activities into immersive and engaging experiences.

Are you ready to unleash your inner gamer, artist, or hobbyist in the Metaverse? It's not just about entertainment; it's about embracing your passions and talents in ways you've never imagined. Let's delve into how the Metaverse elevates your leisure time and allows you to pursue your hobbies and interests with enthusiasm.

Gaming Adventures Await:

In the Metaverse, gaming isn't just a pastime; it's a thrilling adventure that awaits you. Here's how the digital wonderland of the Metaverse opens up boundless gaming possibilities:

Endless Worlds to Conquer:

Imagine stepping into a realm where the boundaries of reality dissolve, and the universe of gaming expands without limits. In the Metaverse, you have access to an infinite array of gaming experiences. Whether you're an explorer, strategist, action hero, or creative visionary, there's a virtual world tailored to your desires. Dive into epic quests to save kingdoms, mastermind strategic victories, engage in pulse-pounding battles, or craft your own virtual empire. It's like having every type of game imaginable at your fingertips, with the added excitement of uncharted adventures.

Connect and Compete:

Gaming in the Metaverse isn't a solitary pursuit; it's a social experience that connects you with players from around the globe. Team up with friends, form alliances, and embark on cooperative missions.

Alternatively, challenge your gaming prowess by competing against players in thrilling esports tournaments. Join vibrant gaming communities where you can share tips, strategies, and experiences, or simply make new friends who share your passion for gaming. It's like having a worldwide network of fellow gamers who are ready to embark on epic quests and forge unforgettable memories.

Pursuing Hobbies and Passions:

Unleash Your Artistic Vision: For artists, the Metaverse is a digital canvas that stretches beyond the horizon. Here, you can create, paint, sculpt, and design with the freedom to explore new dimensions of your craft. Whether you're a traditional painter, a digital artist, or a sculptor, the Metaverse provides you with tools and environments to bring your creative vision to life. It's like having an art studio with an infinite palette, where your imagination knows no bounds.

Collaboration and Exhibition: The Metaverse is more than just a personal creative space; it's a global stage where artists collaborate, exhibit, and inspire. Collaborate with artists from diverse backgrounds, blend your styles, and create groundbreaking artworks together. Showcase your creations in virtual galleries, allowing art enthusiasts from around the world to admire and celebrate your talent. It's like participating in an ongoing international art exhibition that never closes its doors.

Learning and Perfecting Skills:

Mastering Your Hobbies: Hobbies are more than just pastimes; they're opportunities for growth and self-expression. In the Metaverse, you can embark on a journey of learning and mastery in your chosen hobbies. Join hobbyist communities where you can exchange knowledge, tips, and experiences with like-minded individuals. Take virtual lessons from experts, and practice your skills in immersive digital spaces designed to enhance your expertise. Whether you're strumming virtual guitars, experimenting with culinary delights, or nurturing digital gardens, the Metaverse empowers you to elevate your hobbies to new heights. It's like having a playground for your passions, where each day brings new discoveries and achievements.

Are you inspired to transform your hobbies and passions into remarkable adventures in the Metaverse? It's a world where your creativity is boundless, where you can connect with fellow enthusiasts, and where your hobbies become a journey of personal growth and fulfillment. In the upcoming sections, we'll continue to uncover how the Metaverse can enrich your life, from social connections to health and wellness. What hobby or creative pursuit ignites your enthusiasm, and how do you envision exploring it in this digital wonderland? Turn the page, and let's keep unlocking the magic of the Metaverse together!

Chapter 9: Challenges and Concerns

As we continue our journey through the Metaverse, it's important to acknowledge that this digital wonderland isn't without its challenges and concerns. Just like in the physical world, the Metaverse presents its own set of complexities. In this chapter, we'll delve into two critical topics: privacy and security in the Metaverse and how to cope with the potential for addiction. It's vital to navigate these digital waters with awareness and caution while still enjoying the transformative potential of this extraordinary realm.

Are you ready to explore the darker corners of the Metaverse, shed light on potential pitfalls, and find ways to safeguard your digital well-being? Our journey isn't just about the sunny side of this digital wonderland; it's also about ensuring that your experience remains safe, secure, and balanced. Let's dive into the challenges and concerns that you should be aware of while continuing to unlock the magic of the Metaverse.

9.1 Privacy and Security in the Metaverse

Protecting Your Digital Self:

Your digital self is a treasure in the Metaverse, and safeguarding it is paramount. Here's how you can take charge of your privacy and security in this digital wonderland:

Managing Personal Data:

In the Metaverse, your personal data is currency. Just like you wouldn't hand out your wallet to strangers, it's vital to control what you share online. Be cautious about sharing personal information such as your full name, address, phone number, and financial details. Review privacy settings on platforms and apps, and only grant permissions that are necessary. It's like keeping your most valuable possessions locked away safely.

Digital Surveillance Awareness:

Digital surveillance exists in the Metaverse, and understanding how it works is your first line of defense. Be aware that your online activities may be tracked, analyzed, and used for various purposes.

This knowledge empowers you to make informed decisions about what you share and where you go in the digital realm. It's like having a guide through the digital wilderness, helping you avoid potential pitfalls.

Maintaining Control:

In the Metaverse, you're in the driver's seat. Take advantage of privacy tools and practices to maintain control over your virtual presence. Utilize features like privacy settings, encryption, and secure connections to protect your data. Regularly review and update your online profiles and permissions to ensure they align with your preferences. It's like having a fortress with strong gates and vigilant guards.

By managing your personal data, being aware of digital surveillance, and maintaining control over your virtual identity, you can explore the Metaverse confidently, knowing that your digital self is well-protected. How do you plan to implement these practices to ensure your privacy and security in this digital wonderland? Your journey to becoming a digital guardian starts here.

Building Secure Habits:

In the Metaverse, just as in the physical world, building secure habits is essential for a safe and enjoyable experience. Here's how you can establish practices that fortify your digital defenses:

Strong Passwords:
Your digital castle's first line of defense is a strong password. Create unique and complex passwords for your accounts, incorporating a mix of uppercase and lowercase letters, numbers, and special characters. Avoid using easily guessable information like birthdays or common words. Consider using a reputable password manager to keep your credentials secure. It's like having an unbreakable lock on your virtual door.

Two-Factor Authentication (2FA):

Adding an extra layer of security is as easy as enabling two-factor authentication (2FA). With 2FA, even if someone obtains your password, they won't be able to access your accounts without the second authentication method, typically a one-time code sent to your phone or email. Activate 2FA wherever possible to shield your digital fort from unauthorized entry. It's like having a guard at your castle gate who asks for a secret handshake.

Safe Browsing Practices:

Navigating the digital landscape safely involves practicing cautious browsing habits. Avoid clicking on suspicious links, downloading files from untrustworthy sources, or sharing sensitive information on unencrypted websites. Be skeptical of unsolicited emails and messages, as they may be phishing attempts. It's like wearing armor to protect yourself from online threats.

Regular Software Updates:

Keeping your software, operating systems, and antivirus programs up to date is crucial. Updates often include security patches that address vulnerabilities. Regularly install these updates to strengthen your digital fortifications. It's like reinforcing the walls of your castle to withstand attacks.

By incorporating these habits into your digital routine, you'll be well-prepared to navigate the Metaverse securely. How do you plan to implement these practices to ensure your digital safety and peace of mind? Your journey to becoming a vigilant guardian of your digital presence continues, one secure step at a time.

9.2 Coping with Potential Addiction

Recognizing the Signs:

In the immersive world of the Metaverse, it's important to recognize the signs of potential addiction. Here's how you can identify when your digital engagement might be veering into problematic territory:

Change in Priorities:

One of the earliest signs is a shift in your priorities. If you find that you're neglecting real-world responsibilities, such as work, relationships, or self-care, in favor of spending excessive time in the Metaverse, it's time to take notice. Your virtual adventures should complement, not overshadow, your daily life.

Loss of Control:

Losing control over your time and usage is another red flag. If you struggle to set limits on your Metaverse activities or repeatedly find yourself spending more time than intended, it's a sign that your digital engagement may be becoming compulsive.

Withdrawal Symptoms:

Experiencing discomfort or restlessness when you're away from the Metaverse can indicate a potential issue. If you feel anxious, irritable, or constantly thinking about returning to the virtual world, it's time to evaluate your digital habits.

Impact on Well-Being:

Consider how your Metaverse engagement affects your well-being. If it leads to negative consequences in your physical or mental health, such as disrupted sleep patterns, increased stress, or a decline in overall happiness, it's a sign that your digital usage may be problematic.

Isolation and Neglected Relationships:

The Metaverse should enhance your social connections, not replace them. If you're isolating yourself from real-world friends and family or neglecting important relationships because of your digital activities, it's a clear indicator of imbalance.

Decline in Real-World Activities:

A reduction in real-world activities that once brought you joy—such as hobbies, exercise, or outdoor adventures—in favor of virtual engagements can be a sign of excessive digital involvement.

By being aware of these signs, you can proactively evaluate your digital engagement and make adjustments to ensure that your time in the Metaverse remains a positive and balanced experience. How do you plan to recognize and address these signs to maintain a healthy relationship with the digital wonderland of the Metaverse?

Strategies for Balance:

Maintaining balance between your life in the Metaverse and your real-world commitments is key to a healthy and fulfilling experience. Here are effective strategies to ensure you strike that balance:

Set Clear Boundaries:

Establish clear boundaries for your Metaverse activities. Determine specific times when you'll engage in virtual experiences and stick to those schedules. Communicate your boundaries with friends and family, so they understand your availability.

Prioritize Real-World Responsibilities:

Always prioritize your real-world responsibilities. Maintain a daily routine that includes work, chores, exercise, and personal time. Allocate the majority of your day to these essential tasks, leaving defined slots for Metaverse exploration.

Use Technology Wisely:

Leverage technology to your advantage. Set timers or use productivity apps to help you stay on track with your schedule. These tools can remind you to take breaks, switch tasks, or log off when it's time to focus on real-world activities.

Engage in Real-World Activities:

Make a conscious effort to engage in real-world activities that bring you joy and relaxation. Reconnect with hobbies, exercise, spend time with loved ones, and embrace outdoor adventures. Balancing your life with these activities keeps you grounded.

Seek Support and Accountability:

Share your digital journey with friends or family members who can provide support and hold you accountable. They can help remind you of your commitments and encourage you to maintain a healthy balance.

Practice Mindfulness:

Mindfulness techniques can help you stay present in both the digital and real worlds. Engage in meditation, deep breathing exercises, or other mindfulness practices to reduce stress and increase self-awareness.

Set Realistic Goals:

Define achievable goals for your Metaverse adventures. Whether it's completing a certain quest, reaching a specific level, or experiencing particular virtual events, having clear goals can help you maintain a sense of purpose.

Regularly Evaluate and Adjust:

Periodically assess your digital engagement. Reflect on whether your Metaverse activities are enhancing or detracting from your overall well-being. Adjust your strategies and boundaries as needed to maintain balance.

By incorporating these strategies into your digital routine, you can enjoy the Metaverse to the fullest while ensuring that it complements, rather than disrupts, your real-world life. How do you plan to implement these practices to achieve a harmonious

balance in your Metaverse journey?

Chapter 10: Future of the Metaverse

As we conclude our journey through the Metaverse, we stand on the precipice of an ever-expanding digital frontier. In this final chapter, we'll gaze into the crystal ball of possibilities and explore the future of the Metaverse. It's a realm where innovation knows no bounds, and where seniors, too, play an integral role. Join us as we delve into the Metaverse's continued evolution and ponder what lies ahead for seniors in this captivating digital realm.

Can you feel the excitement in the air as we peer into the digital horizon? The Metaverse's future is a world waiting to be woven, and you are an essential part of this narrative. Let's embark on a journey of curiosity and wonder as we explore the potential directions this digital wonderland may take. What changes, innovations, and possibilities do you envision for the Metaverse? How will seniors continue to shape and be shaped by this dynamic digital landscape?

10.1 The Metaverse's Continued Evolution

Innovation Unleashed:

The Metaverse is a canvas where innovation paints its most vivid strokes, and the future promises an even more breathtaking masterpiece. Here's a glimpse of the innovations poised to reshape the Metaverse:

Hyper-Realistic Virtual Worlds:
Imagine stepping into virtual worlds that are virtually indistinguishable from reality. Advancements in graphics, rendering, and processing power are driving the creation of hyper-realistic environments. These digital realms will offer immersive experiences that blur the line between the virtual and the physical, taking realism to astonishing new heights.

Expanded Interactivity:

The future Metaverse isn't just about watching; it's about participating. Enhanced interactivity will enable users to manipulate virtual objects with unprecedented precision, whether it's building virtual structures, crafting intricate designs, or conducting lifelike simulations. The Metaverse will become a playground for creativity and innovation.

Seamless Collaboration:

Virtual collaboration will be seamless, allowing people from around the world to work together in shared virtual spaces. Imagine collaborating on a project with colleagues, brainstorming ideas with friends, or attending a virtual conference—all while feeling like you're in the same room. The Metaverse will break down geographical barriers and foster global collaboration.

AI-Powered Personalization:

Artificial intelligence (AI) will be your digital companion, personalizing your Metaverse experience. AI algorithms will understand your preferences, anticipate your needs, and create tailored content and interactions. It's like having a virtual assistant who knows you inside out.

Virtual Reality Travel:

Travel the world virtually, exploring destinations and cultures from the comfort of your home. Virtual tourism will offer immersive experiences that let you walk through ancient ruins, hike in exotic landscapes, and savor global cuisines—all without leaving your digital avatar.

The Metaverse's future is a canvas where innovation paints the most vivid strokes. How do you envision these advancements shaping your digital adventures in the Metaverse? What hyper-realistic experiences are you most excited to explore? The horizon of possibilities stretches beyond imagination, and you are at the forefront of this exciting journey.

Digital Communities:

In the evolving landscape of the Metaverse, digital communities are like vibrant, interconnected neighborhoods bustling with life and activity. Here's a glimpse of how these communities will shape the future:

Shared Interests, Boundless Connections:
Digital communities within the Metaverse are not limited by geographical constraints. Seniors will have the opportunity to connect with like-minded individuals from around the world who share their interests, hobbies, and passions. Whether it's a virtual art club, a gardening collective, or a community of history enthusiasts, the Metaverse

brings people together based on their common affinities.

Lifelong Learning Hubs:

Imagine a virtual library or university where seniors can engage in continuous learning. Digital communities will offer a wealth of educational resources, from online classes and tutorials to interactive lectures and workshops. Seniors can explore new subjects, acquire new skills, and embark on intellectual journeys, all within the Metaverse's stimulating environment.

Wellness and Support Networks:

Digital communities will foster holistic well-being, providing spaces for seniors to focus on their health and emotional needs. Whether it's participating in virtual yoga sessions, connecting with mental health support groups, or sharing wellness tips, the Metaverse will be a place where seniors can prioritize their physical and emotional wellness.

Creativity and Expression:

The Metaverse empowers seniors to unleash their creativity. Communities centered around the arts, music, writing, and other forms of expression will thrive. Seniors can collaborate on creative projects, showcase their talents, and find inspiration in the company of fellow artists.

Intergenerational Bonds:

One of the most remarkable aspects of digital communities in the Metaverse is the potential for intergenerational connections. Seniors can interact with younger generations, sharing wisdom, experiences, and stories. These interactions bridge generational gaps, foster empathy, and create a rich tapestry of shared knowledge.

Supportive Environments:

Digital communities will prioritize inclusivity and support, ensuring that seniors feel valued and heard. These spaces will be designed to accommodate various abilities and preferences, making them accessible to a diverse senior population.

The Metaverse's digital communities are not just virtual spaces; they are vibrant, welcoming neighborhoods where seniors can connect, learn, create, and thrive. How do you envision yourself participating in these digital communities? What interests or passions would you like to explore and share within the Metaverse's social fabric? The future is ripe with possibilities, and you're invited to join this dynamic tapestry of digital connections.

10.2 What Lies Ahead for Seniors

Senior-Centric Metaverse:

In the evolving landscape of the Metaverse, seniors play a pivotal role, and the digital realm adapts to cater to their unique needs and aspirations. Here's a glimpse of what a senior-centric Metaverse could look like:

Wellness-Oriented Experiences:

The Metaverse becomes a hub for promoting senior well-being. Virtual spaces offer wellness programs tailored to seniors, including guided meditation, low-impact exercise routines, mental health support groups, and nutritional guidance. Seniors can embark on a holistic journey to improve their physical and emotional health within the Metaverse.

Lifelong Learning Opportunities:

The Metaverse becomes a global classroom, offering a diverse range of educational experiences. Seniors have access to online classes, tutorials, and interactive lectures on a multitude of subjects. Learning becomes a lifelong pursuit, empowering seniors to acquire new skills, explore passions, and stay intellectually engaged.

Digital Art and Creativity:

Virtual art studios, music spaces, and writing communities thrive within the Metaverse. Seniors can unleash their creative potential, collaborate with fellow artists, and showcase their work to a global audience. It's a place where artistic expression knows no bounds, and creativity flourishes.

Supportive Social Networks:

Digital communities dedicated to seniors' interests and needs flourish. These communities offer not only social interaction but also emotional support. Seniors can connect with peers who share their experiences, fostering a sense of belonging and camaraderie.

Age-Friendly Design:

Virtual spaces within the Metaverse are thoughtfully designed to accommodate seniors. User interfaces are intuitive, and accessibility features cater to various abilities. The Metaverse becomes an inclusive environment where seniors of all backgrounds can navigate with ease.

Empowerment and Independence:

The Metaverse empowers seniors to maintain their independence. Through virtual assistance, smart homes, and wearable technologies, seniors can manage their daily lives with ease and confidence.

A senior-centric Metaverse is a place where seniors can live, learn, create, and connect on their terms. It's a digital realm that recognizes and celebrates the contributions of seniors, ensuring they continue to lead fulfilling lives. How do you envision your role in a senior-centric Metaverse, and what experiences are you most excited to explore and create within this dynamic digital landscape?

Interconnected Generations:

One of the most transformative aspects of the Metaverse is its ability to bridge generational divides and create connections between people of all ages. Here's how interconnected generations will shape the Metaverse of the future:

1. Shared Experiences: The Metaverse provides a platform for different generations to share experiences, stories, and perspectives. Seniors can engage with younger generations, and vice versa, in virtual spaces that encourage conversation and understanding.

2. Knowledge Transfer: In the Metaverse, knowledge flows freely between generations. Seniors can pass down their wisdom and experiences to younger individuals, while younger generations can introduce seniors to new technologies and digital trends. It's a dynamic exchange of expertise and innovation.

3. Empathy and Understanding: Interactions between generations foster empathy and understanding. Seniors gain insight into the challenges and opportunities faced by younger individuals, while younger generations gain a deeper appreciation for the experiences and history of their elders.

These interactions break down stereotypes and build stronger connections.

4. Collaborative Projects: The Metaverse facilitates collaborative projects that transcend age barriers. Seniors and younger individuals can work together on creative endeavors, educational initiatives, and community-building efforts. It's a space where diverse skills and perspectives combine to achieve common goals.

5. Digital Family Bonds: Families can create digital hubs within the Metaverse, allowing members of different generations to stay connected regardless of physical distance.

Virtual family gatherings, celebrations, and shared activities become part of everyday life, strengthening familial bonds.

6. Supportive Networks: Seniors can find support and companionship from both their peers and younger individuals in virtual communities. These networks provide emotional support, social engagement, and a sense of belonging.

The Metaverse's power to connect generations creates a vibrant tapestry of shared experiences and collaborative opportunities. It's a place where age is not a barrier but a bridge to deeper understanding and unity. How do you envision your role in this interconnected world of the Metaverse, and what kinds of experiences or connections are you most eager to explore across generations?

Conclusion

As we reach the end of our journey through the Metaverse for seniors, we find ourselves at the crossroads of possibility and wonder. The Metaverse is not just a digital realm; it's a canvas for creativity, a stage for connections, and a sanctuary for well-being. In this conclusion, we reflect on the transformative potential of the Metaverse for seniors and the boundless opportunities that await.

Reflecting on the Metaverse:
Our exploration began with an overview of the Metaverse—a realm of digital wonders where realities merge, and imagination knows no bounds. We delved into why seniors matter in the Metaverse,

recognizing the invaluable contributions they bring to this dynamic digital landscape.

Navigating the Metaverse:

We navigated the Metaverse, learning how to create digital identities, access virtual spaces, and interact with others. The Metaverse became a place where seniors could not only explore but also express their unique selves.

Benefits for Seniors:

The Metaverse opened doors to health and wellness, combating loneliness and isolation. It provided seniors with virtual healthcare, opportunities for connection, and avenues for personal growth. It became a digital oasis for well-being and fulfillment.

Healthcare in the Metaverse:
We explored the future of healthcare within the Metaverse, from virtual doctor visits to immersive rehabilitation experiences. The Metaverse became a frontier in health and wellness, offering new ways for seniors to care for their physical and mental health.

Social Connections:
Seniors rekindle old friendships, joined virtual social groups, and attended events and gatherings. The Metaverse became a place where social bonds thrived, regardless of physical distance.

Learning and Lifelong Education:

Seniors engaged in online classes, tutorials, and explored virtual museums and historical adventures. The Metaverse transformed into an endless classroom, where learning knows no age limit.

Entertainment and Recreation:

Traveling the world virtually, gaming, and pursuing hobbies and passions became everyday experiences within the Metaverse. It became a realm of boundless entertainment and recreation.

Challenges and Concerns:

We addressed concerns related to privacy, security, and potential addiction, offering strategies for balance and digital guardianship. The Metaverse became a place where seniors could explore safely and responsibly.

Future of the Metaverse:

In the concluding chapter, we glimpsed the Metaverse's future—a world of innovation, interconnected generations, and senior-centric experiences. The Metaverse emerged as a place where seniors would continue to shape and be shaped by its dynamic landscape.

In closing, the Metaverse is not a distant dream; it's a digital frontier waiting to be explored. Seniors, with their wisdom, experiences, and curiosity, are central to this journey. As we embark on this adventure, let's remember that the Metaverse is a canvas for connection, creativity, and community. It's a place where age is just a number, and the possibilities are endless.

The Metaverse is your playground, your sanctuary, and your canvas. How will you paint your digital masterpiece? How will you connect, learn, create, and thrive within its virtual realms? The Metaverse is yours to shape, and the adventure continues. Embrace the future with open arms, for in the Metaverse, there are no limits—only horizons waiting to be explored.

www.ingramcontent.com/pod-product-compliance
Lightning Source LLC
LaVergne TN
LVHW051336050326
832903LV00031B/3566